IS IT A SAINT'S NAME?

OVER 3000
CHRISTIAN NAMES
FOR
GIRLS AND BOYS

WITH A LIST OF
PATRON SAINTS

Compiled by

REV. WILLIAM P. DUNNE

TAN BOOKS AND PUBLISHERS, INC.
Rockford, Illinois 61105

Nihil Obstat
John J. Clifford, S.J.
Censor Deputatus

Imprimatur
Samuel Cardinal Stritch
Archbishop of Chicago

St. Theophilas, March 5, 1948
St. Paschal Baylon, May 17, 1949

TAN BOOKS AND PUBLISHERS, INC.
P.O. Box 424
Rockford, Illinois 61105
1977

FOREWORD

From the early ages the Church has required baptismal names which have a Christian significance. The great number of martyrs, confessors, and holy persons served to swell the list of names. This booklet does not include all the Christian names, old forms and those which sound strange to the modern ear have been omitted. Not all are names of those officially saints. Before the process of canonization was drawn up many persons were venerated as having lived unusually holy lives and custom has established their names as Christian names. Others, such as titles and feasts of the Blessed Virgin, belong in the list. The forms and variations given are accepted variations of Christian names. While this booklet does not include all Christian names, it does represent a studied effort to bring together all names which are in modern usage. It is reasonably safe to conclude that any name, at all common, which is not found herein is not a saint's name.

In choosing baptismal names parents should keep in mind the thought that the child will bear these names throughout life. They should be careful to avoid names or combinations which will subject the bearer to ridicule. Light and fancy-sounding names should not be given to boys; nicknames should not be given in Baptism; given names should be balanced with the surname. The length of the given names should have a harmonious relation to one another and to the family name. A rhythm and cadence of sound should be sought.

Forms and variations derived from ancient names are listed under the original name, or its most popular form.

The date given each name is that assigned as the day upon which the saint may be publicly honored. This day is also called one's "names-day."

When a name differs considerably from the original form, the saint's name is given in parentheses.

Readers will note the unusual number of beautiful and unfamiliar female names. Many charming and euphonious combinations can be formed.

To lessen confusion and mistakes, an increasing need has been felt for names other than the comparatively few among commonly used. Making more Christian names available will increase our knowledge of the great number of saints and holy persons who have given glory to God by their exemplary lives. By assuming these names we honor these persons and through them Almighty God, the Source of all their goodness and virtue. Such names are certainly more becoming to members of the human race redeemed by Jesus Christ than the names of pagan gods, trees, flowers and places.

CHRISTIAN NAMES
GIRLS

— A —

Acacia .... March 29
  Acatia
Acra .... June 8
Ada .... Dec. 4
  Adna, Adonetta
Adamina (Adam) .... Dec. 24
Adavisa .... Aug. 29
Adelaide .... Dec. 16
  Addie, Adelais
  Adelecia, Adleta
Adelina .... Oct. 20
  Adelia, Adeline
Adela .... Feb. 24
  Adel, Adella, Adele, Adeliza
Adilia .... Dec. 13
Adolphina .... June 17
  Adolphine
Adria .... Dec. 2
  Adrianne
Adriana .... Aug. 10
Aemilia (Emilian) .... Sept. 11
  Aemiliana
Aerenia .... March 8
Afra .... Aug. 5
Afrina .... Oct. 21
Agapa .... Aug. 8
Agape .... Feb. 15
Agatha .... Feb. 5
  Agata, Agathe, Aggie
Agnes .... Jan. 21
  Agna, Agne, Agneda,
  Agnella, Agnessa, Agnese
  Agneta, Inez, Ines, Inista,
  Neysa

Aimee .... June 10
  Aime
Alacoque .... Oct. 17
  St. Marg. Mary)
Alane .... Nov. 25
  Alanna
Alaranna .... Nov. 26
Alba .... Jan. 17
Alberta .... March 11
  Albertina, Albertine,
  Albrette
Albina .... Dec. 16
Alcidia .... May 29
Alda .... April 26
Alena .... June 24
Alexandra .... May 18
  Alesandra, Alexandrina,
  Alexandrine, Alexa, Alexine
Alexia .... June 29
  Alexis
Alfonsa .... Aug. 2
  Alphonsina, Alonsa
Alfreda .... Aug. 2
Alfrida .... Dec. 8
Alice (Adelaide) .... Dec. 16
  Alicia, Aline, Alexie,
  Alisa, Allis, Alyce, Alletta
  Alodia, Alyssa, Ilsa
Alma
A title of The Blessed Mother
Alodia .... Oct. 22
Aloysia .... Sept. 12
  Aloys, Aloisia, Aloyza
Alva .... Sept. 11
Alverna .... Sept. 14
  Alvernia, Laverne

Alvina	June	2
Alvira	March	6
Amabilis	Nov.	1
Amabel, Amabella		
Amanda	June	18
Amarna	July	8
Amata	June	10
Ambrosine (Ambrose)	Dec.	7
Amelia	June	2
Amelie		
America (Emmeric)	Nov.	4
Amy (Amata)	June	10
Amicia,		
Anastasia	Dec.	25
Anatolia	July	9
Anatola		
Andrea (Andrew)	Nov.	30
Andrene		
Androna	Nov.	3
Angela	May	31
Ancela, Angele,		
Angelique, Angelita,		
Anjela, Aniela		
Angelina	July	15
Anicia	May	11
Anne	July	26
Anna, Anita, Anitra		
Annabel, Annabelle,		
Annata, Annie, Anusia		
Annunciata	March	25
Feast of the Blessed Mother		
Anselina	April	21
Anselma		
Antigone (Antigonus)	Feb.	27
Antoinette	May	3
Antoinetta, Antonetta		
Antonia	May	13
Antonina	May	3
Anysia	Dec.	30
Anisia, Annice		
Aquila	Jan.	31
Arabia	March	13
Archangela	Feb.	13
Ardalia	April	14
Ariadne	Sept.	17
Ariadna		
Arilda	Oct.	30
Armella	Oct.	24
Arnoldine	March	14
Asteria	Aug.	10
Attracta	Aug.	11
Auberta (Albert)	Nov.	15
Audrey	June	23
Aubrie		
Augusta	March	27
Asta		
Aulaire	Feb.	12
Aura	July	19
Aurea, Goldie		
Aurelia	Dec.	2
Austine	Aug.	28
Ava	April	29
Avida	May	7
Azelle	Dec.	6

— B —

Babette (Elizabeth)	Nov.	5
Babilla	May	20
Balbina	March	31
Baptista	June	24
Barbara	Dec.	4
Barba, Barbe, Barica,		
Barbora		
Bartillia	Jan.	3
Basila	Aug.	29
Basilica	Nov.	29
Basilia	March	13
Basilissa	Jan.	9
Basilla		
Beata	March	8
Beatrice	July	29
Bea, Beatrix		
Belina	Feb.	19
Belinda		
Belle (Isabel)	July	8

Bellina .... Sept. 9
Benedicta .... March 21
  Benedeta, Beneta, Benita,
  Benite, Benoite, Benedetta
Benilda .... June 15
Berenice .... Oct. 4
  Bernice
Berina .... Nov. 26
Bernarda .... May 20
  Bernadette, Bernardina,
  Bernardine
Bertha .... July 4
  Berthel, Bertel
Bertilla .... Jan. 3
  Bertilia, Bertina
Beth .... Dec. 5
Betilda .... Jan. 26
Betty (Elizabeth) .... Nov. 5
Beverley .... May 7
  Beverly
Bibiana .... Dec. 2
Birona .... March 8
Blanche .... July 5
  Bianca, Branca, Blanca
  Blanch
Blandina .... June 2
  Blandine
Bobilia .... Oct. 16
Bonnie .... May 29
Brenda (Brendan) .... May 16
Briana (Brian) .... March 22
Bridget .... Oct. 8
  Bride, Brigette, Brigid,
  Brigitta, Bristta, Brita
Burga (Walburga) .... Feb. 25
Buriana .... June 4

— C —

Calista .... Sept. 2
  Callista
Camelia .... Sept. 16
  Camella

Camilla .... March 3
  Camila, Camille
Candia .... Oct. 22
Candida .... June 6
Canice .... Oct. 11
Careme .... Sept. 7
Carina .... Nov. 7
Carisia .... May 6
Carissima .... Sept. 7
Carita .... June 12
Carmel .... July 16
  Our Lady of Mt. Carmel
  Carmela, Carmelita
  Carmen, Melita
Carmilla .... March 23
Caroline (Charles) .... Nov. 4
  Carla, Carlen, Carleen,
  Carletta, Carlina, Carlinna,
  Carlin, Carlita, Carilla,
  Carol, Carolina, Carrie,
  Charlene, Charlet, Cheryl
Casilda .... April 9
Cassandra (Alexandra) ....May 18
Cassilda .... April 9
Catalina .... May 11
Catharine (Catherine) ....April 30
  Catana, Catania,
  Caterina, Cathleen,
  Katherine, Kathleen,
  Kathryn, Krina, Karen,
  Kathy
Cazaria .... Dec. 8
Cecilia .... Nov. 22
  Caecilia, Cecile, Cecily,
  Celia, Celie, Celine,
  Cicile, Cisily
Celerina .... Feb. 3
Celeste .... April 16
  Celesta
Celestina .... May 10
Cella (Marcella) .... Jan. 31
Cera .... Jan. 5

Cerenna .... Nov. 15
Charity .... Aug. 1
  Charissa, Cherry
Charlotte (Charles) ....Nov. 4
  Carlina, Carlota,
  Carlotta, Charlet
Charmaine .... Jan. 28
  (Charlemagne)
Chiara .... Jan. 5
Christina .... July 24
  Christa, Christabel,
  Christabelle, Christal,
  Christel, Christine,
  Cristina, Crystal, Kerstin
Chrysa .... Aug. 24
Cilinia .... Oct. 21
Cineria .... Oct. 29
Cinthia .... Feb. 8
  Cynthia
Clara .... Aug. 12
  Claire, Clare, Clareta,
  Clarice, Clarinda, Clarine,
  Claribel, Claribelle,
  Clarissa, Clarita, Chiara
Claudia .... May 18
  Claudina, Claudine,
  Claudette
Clementina .... June 5
  Clemency, Clementine
Cleopatra .... Oct. 19
  Cleo
Colette .... March 6
  Coletta, Collette
Colona .... Dec. 31
Columba .... Sept. 17
Columbina .... May 22
  Columbine
Comelia .... April 20
Conception .... Dec. 8
Feast of Our Blessed Mother
The Immaculate Conception.
  Concha, Conchita, Concetta

Concessa .... Apr. 8
Concordia .... Aug. 13
Condita .... Aug. 14
Conradine .... Nov. 26
Constance .... Sept. 19
  Connie, Constancia,
  Constantia
Consuelo
  Title of Blessed Mother
  Our Lady of Consolation
  Consuela, Consolata
Cordelia .... Oct. 22
  Cora, Corinne
Corintha .... Aug. 8
Cornella .... March 31
  Cornelia
Corona .... May 14
Cotilla .... Jan. 23
Credola .... May 13
Crescentia .... June 15
  Crescencia
Crispina .... Dec. 5
Cuthberta .... March 20
Cynthia .... Feb. 8
Cyra .... Aug. 3
Cyrena .... Nov. 1
  Cyrenia
Cyria .... June 5
Cyriaca .... March 20
Cyriana .... Nov. 1
Cyrilla .... Oct. 29
  Cyrille

— D —

Dagila .... July 12
Daire .... Nov. 2
Daisy (Margaret) .... June 10
Damaris .... Oct. 4
  Demara
Damiana .... April 12
Daniela .... July 21
  Danette, Danila, Danita

Daphne .... July 13
Daretia .... July 19
Daria .... Oct. 25
   Darice
Datiana .... May 31
Datina .... Dec. 6
Dauphine .... Nov. 26
Davida .... Dec. 29
   Davina, Vida
Deborah .... Sept. 1
Deidre .... Jan. 15
   Deirdre
Demetria .... June 21
Delia (Cordelia) .... Oct. 22
   Della
Delphine .... Dec. 9
   Delfina, Delphina
Denise (Dennis) .... Nov. 17
   Denice, Denys
Desiree (Desiderius) ...... May 23
   Desirata
Devota .... Jan. 27
Diana .... June 9
   Diane
Didara .... June 23
Digna .... Aug. 11
Dina (Geraldine) .... Oct. 13
Dionysia .... Dec. 12
   Dionetta, Dionisia, Diona
Dolores .... Sept. 15

Title of the Blessed Mother
"Our Lady of Sorrows"

   Delores, Dolora, Dolorita
   Deloris
Domaine .... May 20
Dominica .... July 6
Donalda .... July 15
Donata .... Dec. 31
   Dona, Donna
Dorcas .... Oct. 25
   Dorcea, Dorcia

Dorothy .... Feb. 6
   Dora, Doralia, Doralice,
   Doralis, Doralise, Dore,
   Dorea, Dorelia, Dorena,
   Doretta, Dorette, Doria,
   Dorice, Dorinda, Dorinna,
   Doris, Dorissa, Dorita,
   Dorlisa, Dorna, Dorothea,
   Dot, Dotty, Dolly
Drusilla .... Sept. 22
   Drucilla
Dulcelina .... Oct. 26
   Dulcea, Dulcia, Dulcie,
   Dulcina, Dulcyna
Dympna .... May 15

      — E —

Eberta (Egbert) .... April 24
Edana .... July 5
Edberga .... June 15
Eden (Aedan) .... May 2
Edith .... Sept. 16
   Edita, Editha, Edyth
Edmunda .... Nov. 20
   Edmee, Edmonda
Edna (Edana) .... July 5
Edwarda .... Oct. 13
   Edwardina, Edwardine
Edwina .... Oct. 12
Egberta .... April 24
Egena .... May 18
Eileen (Helen) .... Aug. 18
Elaine (Helen) .... Aug. 18
Eleanor .... Aug. 16
   Eleanora, Eleanore,
   Eleonor, Lena, Nora
Electa .... Oct. 21
Elena .... Nov. 4
Elenara .... May 2
Elene (Helen) .... Aug. 18
Elevara .... March 28
Elevetha .... Aug. 1

Elfrida .... Dec. 8
  Elfreda
Elia .... Oct. 25
Elizabeth .... Nov. 5
  Bess, Beta, Beth, Betha,
  Betina, Betsey, Betta,
  Bettina, Betty, Elisa,
  Elisabet, Elisabetta, Elise,
  Elisia, Elissa, Eliza, Elsa,
  Elsabet, Elsbeth, Elspeth,
  Elna, Elora, Helsa, Libby,
  Lisa, Lisbeth
Ella .... Oct. 27
  Elletta, Ellette
Ellen (Helen) .... Aug. 18
Elma .... April 15
Eloine (Eloi) .... Dec. 1
Eloise (Louise) .... Jan. 31
Elsie (Elizabeth) .... Nov. 5
Elvara .... March 28
Elvira .... Jan. 25
Emelia .... May 23
Emeline .... Oct. 27
Emerentiana .... Jan. 23
  Emerentia
Emily .... Sept. 19
  Emelin, Emelina, Emeline,
  Emelyn, Emilie, Emmelia,
  Emmeline
Emma .... Apr. 11
Enid .... Aug. 1
Enora .... April 12
Enrica (Henry) .... July 15
  Enrika
Erena .... May 5
Erica (Eric) .... May 18
  Erika
Ermelinda .... Oct. 29
  Erma, Irma, Linda
Ernestina .... Nov. 7
  Erna, Ernesta, Ernestine
Esperanza (Hope) .... Aug. 1

Esperance
Esprite .... Aug. 7
Estelle .... May 21
  Stella
Esther .... July 1
  Easter, Esthera, Estra,
  Estrella
Etha .... May 5
Ethel .... Jan. 12
  Ethelina
Ethelviva .... June 25
Etta (Henry) .... July 15
Eudocia .... March 1
  Eudosia
Eudoxia .... Nov. 2
Eugenia .... Dec. 15
  Eugenie
Eulalia .... Feb. 12
  Eulalie
Eunice .... Oct. 28
Euphemia .... March 20
  Effie
Euralia .... Dec. 10
Eurosia .... June 25
Eustella .... May 21
  Eustelle
Euthalia .... Aug. 27
Eutropia .... Dec. 14
Eve .... May 26
Evangelista .... Sept. 16
  Evangeline
Eve .... Dec. 19
  Aveline, Evelina,
  Eveline, Evelien, Evelyn,
  Lena, Lina

— F —

Fabia .... Jan. 20
  Fabiana, Fabienne
Fabiola .... Dec. 27
Faila .... March 3
Faina .... May 18

Faith .... Aug. 1
   Fay, Faye, Fayette
Fanchea .... Jan. 1
Fanchette (Frances) .... Oct. 4
   Fanchon
Fara .... April 3
Farica .... July 18
Faustina .... Jan. 18
   Fausta, Faustine
Fedora (Theodora) .... April 1
Fedosia (Theodosia) ...... April 2
Felicia .... Oct. 5
   Felice, Felise, Felita
Felicita .... March 6
Felipa (Philippa) .... Sept. 20
   Filipa, Felisa
Fenella .... Nov. 13
Ferdinanda .... May 30
   Fernanda, Fernande
Fidelia .... March 23
Fidelity (Fidelis) .... April 24
Fifi (Josephine) .... Oct. 23
Flavia .... May 7
Flora .... Nov. 24
   Florella, Floretta, Floria,
   Floris, Flossie
Florence .... Nov. 10
   Florencia, Florentia,
   Florinda, Flossie
Florentina .... June 20
Floreta .... Aug. 22
Florida .... Aug. 29
Florina .... May 1
Flotilda .... Dec. 25
Fonilla .... Jan. 17
Fortuna .... Feb. 22
   Fortune
Fortunata .... Oct. 14
Fortunia .... April 27
Franca .... April 27
Frances .... March 9
   Fanchette, Fanchon,

Fanchonette, Fanny, France,
   Francella, Francesca,
   Francine, Francisca,
   Franny
Francha .... April 25
Freda (Fredrick) .... July 18
   Fredella, Frederica,
   Fredrika, Freida, Frida,
   Fritzi

— G —

Gabriella .... March 24
   Gabrielle, Gavrila,
   Gabriele, Gabriela
Gadola .... May 6
Gaiana .... Sept. 30
Gaiola .... March 3
Galalia .... Dec. 10
Galata .... April 19
Galena .... Feb. 10
Galla .... Oct. 5
Galonia .... July 24
Garda (Hildegarde) .... April 30
Gavina .... May 6
Gemina .... Jan. 4
Gemma .... April 11
Generosa .... July 17
Genesia .... Aug. 25
Genevieve .... Jan. 3
   Genever, Genevra,
   Guinevere, Ginevra,
   Geneva
Genoise .... Dec. 23
Gentile .... Jan. 28
Georgia .... Feb. 15
   Georgetta, Georgette,
   Georgiana, Georgina,
   Georgine
Geralda .... March 13
   Geraldina, Geraldine,
   Gerelda, Gerlinda,
   Giralda

Gerberta .... Dec. 19
Germaine .... June 15
Gertrude .... Nov. 16
   Gertruda, Gerty, Trude,
   Trudy
Gilberta (Gilberte) .... Feb. 4
Gilda (Gildas) .... Jan. 29
Gisele .... May 7
   Giselle, Gisella
Gladys .... March 29
Gloria .... May 10
   Gloriana, Glorianna, Glory
Glyceria .... May 13
   Glitheria, Glycere
Godeleva .... July 6
   Godelieva, Godelieve
Godina .... Feb. 15
Golinia .... July 6
Gorgonia .... Dec. 9
Grace .... July 5
   Gracia, Gratia, Gratiana
Graecina .... June 16
Grata .... May 1
Gredel (Margaret) .... June 10
Gregoria .... Nov. 17
Gresinda .... July 25
Greta (Margaret) .... June 10
   Gretchen, Grethel, Grita
Guadalupe .... Dec. 12
   Famous Mexican Shrine of
    Our Lady of Guadalupe
   Lupe
Gudela (Gudelia) .... Sept. 29
Guenna .... Aug. 19
Guenevere (Genevieve) .... Jan. 3
Guida (Guy) .... Sept. 12
Guilette (William) .... June 25
   Guillena
Guiteria .... May 22

Gwen .... July 5
   Gwenn
Gwendolene .... Oct. 18
   Gwendolen, Gwendolin,
   Gwendoline, Gwendolyn
Gytha .... Feb. 15

— H —

Haberilla .... Jan. 30
   Habrilla
Halena .... June 17
Hallie (Henry) .... July 15
   Hally
Hannah (Anne) .... July 26
Harolda (Harold) .... March 25
   Harelda
Harriet (Henry) .... July 15
   Hariett, Harrietta,
   Hattie, Hatty
Hedwig .... Oct. 17
   Hedda, Hedy
Heira .... Feb. 21
Helen .... Aug. 18
   Aileen, Eileen, Elaine,
   Ellen, Ellin, Ellyn, Helena,
   Helene, Helenka, Ilona,
   Ilsa, Ilse, Lena, Lenora,
   Lenore, Leona, Leonora,
   Leonore, Pamela
Helia .... June 20
   Heliada
Heliana .... June 8
Heliena .... April 20
Helmina (William) .... June 25
Heloise (Louise) .... Jan. 31
Helsa (Elizabeth) .... Nov. 5
Henrica (Henry) .... July 15
   Hendrica, Henrika, Henrita,
   Henryka, Henrietta,
   Henriette, Henrieta, Hetty
Heraclia .... June 1

Herena .... Feb. 25	
Herene	
Herenia .... March 8	
Herina .... May 5	
Herlanda .... Mar. 22	
Hermana (Herman) .... Apr. 7	
Hermandine, Hermine	
Hermione .... Sept. 4	
Hermia, Herminia	
Hero .... Jan. 18	
Hesperia .... Aug. 10	
Hester (Esther) .... July 1	
Hilaria .... Aug. 12	
Hilda .... Nov. 17	
Hildeberta .... Apr. 4	
Hildeburg .... June 3	
Hildegard .... Sept. 17	
Hildegarda, Hildegarde,	
Hulda	
Hildemara .... Oct. 25	
Hiltrude .... Sept. 27	
Hirena .... Feb. 25	
Hirmina .... Dec. 24	
Honesta .... Oct. 18	
Honora .... Apr. 12	
Honore	
Honorata .... Jan. 11	
Honoria .... Apr. 12	
Hope .... Aug. 1	
Esperanza, Nadine	
Horta (Dorothy) .... Feb. 6	
Hortense .... Jan. 11	
Huberta (Hubert) .... Nov. 3	
Huette (Hugh) .... Apr. 29	
Huguetta, Hugette	
Hulda .... Apr. 10	
Humbelina .... Feb. 12	
Humbeline	
Humility .... May 22	
Hyacinth .... Jan. 30	
Hyacintha, Hyacinthe	
Hypatia .... June 17	

— I —

Iacolyn (James) .... July 25
Ida .... Sept. 4
  Idelle, Idette
Idea .... Jan. 15
Ignatia .... Feb. 1
  Ignacia
Illuminata .... Nov. 29
Ilsa (Helen) .... Aug. 18
  Ilse, Ilona
Imelda .... May 12
Immaculata .... Dec. 8

*Feast of the Immaculate
Conception*

Imogene .... Sept. 8

*Shrine of Blessed Virgin,
at Imoge, France*

  Imogen
Imperia .... Sept. 6
Indica .... May 9
Inez .... Nov. 8
  Ines
Ingrid .... July 1
  Inga
Innocensia .... Feb. 1
  Innocentia
Iolana (Yolando) .... Dec. 28
  Iolanda
Ionilla .... Jan. 17
Iphigenia .... Sept. 21
Iraidea .... Sept. 5
Irene .... Oct. 20
  Irena, Irina, Renie
Irmina .... Dec. 24
  Irma
Isabel .... July 8
  Belita, Belle, Isabeau,
  Isabella, Isabelle,
  Isbel, Isobel
Isadora .... Apr. 4
  Isidora

Ita .... Jan. 15
Ite .... Jan. 15
Iva .... Oct. 27
Ivanna (John) .... Dec. 27
Ivetta .... Jan. 13
   Iveta, Ivette, Ivy
Ivona (Yvonne) .... May 19

— J —

Jacinta (Hyacinth) .... Jan. 30
   Jacintha, Jacinthe
Jacobina .... Aug. 1
   Jacobia
Jacqueline (James) .... July 25
   Jacobella, Jacquetta,
   Jaculin, Jamesina, Jamesine
Jane .... Aug. 21
   Janel, Janella, Janet,
   Janette, Janetta, Janice,
   Johanna, Juanita
Janilla .... Jan. 17
Januaria .... Feb. 11
Jean (Joanna) .... May 24
   Jeanette, Jenifer, Jeanie,
   Jeanne
Jeonilla .... Jan. 17
Jeremia .... Jan. 21
Jessica (Joanna) .... May 24
   Jessie
Jill (Julia) .... May 22
Joan .... May 30
Jobina (Job) .... May 10
Jocelyn .... Mar. 17
   Jocelin, Joceline, Josslyn
Jocunda .... June 2
Johanna .... May 24
   Henchen
Jolenta .... Mar. 6
Joletta (Viola) .... May 3
   Jolietta
Jonella .... Jan. 16
   Jonila

Josepha .... Feb. 14
Josephine .... Oct. 23
   Josephina, Giuseppa
Jovita .... Feb. 15
Joy (Jucunda) .... July 27
Joyce (Jucunda) .... July 27
Juana .... Dec. 8
Juanita .... Aug. 21
Jucunda .... July 27
Judith .... Sept. 14
   Juditha, Judithe, Judy
Julia .... May 22
   Julchen, Jule, Joli,
   Juliana, Juliane, Julianna,
   Julianne, Juliet, Julietta,
   Julita
Juliana .... June 19
Julie .... July 12
Juliette .... May 18
Julitta .... June 16
June (Junia) .... Nov. 14
Junella .... Jan. 17
Junilla .... Feb. 16
Justa .... July 19
Justilla .... Aug. 28
Justina .... Apr. 14
   Justine

— K —

Karen (Katherine) .... April 30
   Kara, Karena, Kalina,
   Karin, Karina, Kasia,
   Kassia, Katrina, Katherine,
   Kathleen, Katheryn,
   Katarina, Katinka, Katrien,
   Kitty
Karla (Charles) .... Nov. 4
Karoline .... Nov. 4
Kayne .... Oct. 8
Kennera .... Oct. 29
Kenwyn .... Oct. 8
Kerstin (Christiana) .... July 24
   Kirstie, Kisten, Kristina

Keverne .... Nov. 18
Keyna .... Oct. 8
Kilda .... Nov. 1
Kim Korean Martyrs
Kinga .... July 24

— L —

Lamberta .... Sept. 17
  Lambertina, Lambertine
Lancia .... Aug. 18
Landine .... Jan. 16
  Landoline
Languida .... Oct. 21
Latina .... June 2
Laura .... Oct. 19
  Laure, Laurena, Laurene,
  Laureen, Lauretta, Laurette,
  Laurine, Laurice, Lorita,
  Lora, Loris, Laurinda
Laurentina .... Oct. 8
  Laurentia
Laverne .... Sept. 17
  LaVerne, Lavernne,
  Alvernia
Lea (Leah) .... Mar. 22
Leda .... Mar. 27
Lee (Elizabeth) .... Nov. 5
Legissima .... Apr. 27
Lelia .... Aug. 11
Lelica .... Feb. 12
  Lela
Lena (Helen) .... Aug. 18
  Lenchen, Lenia
Lene .... Nov. 12
Lenora (Helen) .... Aug. 18
  Lenore, Leon, Leora
  Lonie, Lora, Leonora
Leona (Leo) .... Apr. 11
  Leola, Leonie
Leonarda .... Nov. 26
Leonice .... Mar. 1

Leonilla .... Jan. 17
Leonita .... Mar. 1
  Leontina, Leontine
Leopolda .... Apr. 2
  Leopoldina
Letitia .... Dec. 25
  Leticia, Letty
Libaria .... Oct. 8
Libera .... Jan. 18
Liberta .... Jan. 16
Liberty .... Feb. 3
Libya .... June 25
Liceria .... May 11
Lidia .... Mar. 27
Lillian .... July 27
  Lila, Lili, Lilah,
  Liley, Lilia, Lilis, Lilisa,
  Lillie, Lillien, Lillis, Lilly
Lina .... Aug. 18
Linda (Ermelinda) .... Oct. 29
Lisa (Elizabeth) .... Nov. 5
  Lise, Lisetta, Lisette,
  Lisi, Lisbeth
Lois .... Jan. 31
Lola .... Jan. 31
Lolita (Dolores) .... Sept. 15
  Loleta
Lollia .... June 23
  Lollie
Lora (Laura) .... Oct. 19
Loraine (Laurentia) .... Oct. 8
Lorena .... Aug. 10
  Lorna
Lorenza .... Oct. 8
Loretta .... Dec. 10
    Shrine of Our Lady of
    Loretta (Italy)
Lottie (Charlotte) .... Nov. 4
  Lotta
Louise .... Jan. 31
  Lois, Lou, Louison,
  Lulu, Lola

Lourdes .... Feb. 11
Famous Shrine of Our Lady of Lourdes. (France)
Lucasta .... June 27
Lucella .... May 10
Luchina .... Aug. 23
Luciana .... May 18
Lucida .... Jan. 3
Lucilla .... June 29
Lucina .... June 30
Lucinia .... May 25
Lucosa .... Sept. 28
Lucretia .... Nov. 23
    Lucrece
Lucy .... Dec. 13
    Lucasta, Luce, Lucilla,
    Lucia, Luciana, Lucie,
    Lucetta, Lucille, Lucina,
    Lucinda, Lucya
Ludmilla .... Sept. 16
Ludovica .... Jan. 31
Luella (Louise-Ella) ...... Aug. 25
    Louella
Luisa .... Jan. 31
    Luise, Luiza
Lunette .... Aug. 1
Lupe (Guadalupe) .... Dec. 12
Lydia .... Aug. 3
    Lidia

— M —

Mabilia .... Nov. 21
    Mabele, Mabelle, Maybelle
Mabel (Mabilia) .... Nov. 21
Macaria .... Apr. 8
    Macaire
Macra .... Jan. 6
Macrina .... Jan. 14
Madalena (Magdalen) .... July 22
Madeleine .... July 17
Magda (Margaret) .... June 10
Magdalene .... July 22

Madalene, Madeline,
Madalyn, Madel, Madelon,
Magdala, Magdalen,
Magdalene, Magdelaine,
Malina, Marlina, Marlene
Madonna .... Oct. 11
In honor of The Blessed Mother of Our Lord Jesus Christ.
Magina .... Dec. 3
Magita .... Sept. 8
Magna .... May 6
Majella .... Oct. 16
    (St. Gerard Majella)
Malina .... Apr. 28
Mandie (Amanda) .... June 18
    Manda
Manon (Mary) .... Dec. 8
    Manette
Manuelita (Manuel) .... June 17
    Manuela
Marana .... Aug. 3
Marca (Mark) .... April 25
    Marcel, Marcele, Marcelle,
Marcella .... Jan. 31
    Marcel, Marcele, Marcelle,
    Marcellina
Marchell .... Sept. 5
Marcia .... March 3
Marciana .... May 24
Marcina .... June 8
Mardia .... Oct. 22
Marella .... May 21
Mareme .... Nov. 22
Marga .... April 6
Margaret .... June 10
    Madge, Magde, Marfa,
    Margareta, Margarita,
    Margarta, Margery, Margo,
    Margory, Marjory, Margala,
    Margola, Marsali, Maggie,

Gret, Greta, Gretchen,
Grethel, Gretel, Pearl,
Peggy, Maisie, Reta
Marianna .... April 17
Mariana, Marianne
Marina .... June 18
Marita .... March 16
Marsilia .... April 8
Martana .... Dec. 2
Martha .... July 29
Marta, Martel, Martella,
Marthine
Martia .... June 21
Martina .... Jan. 30
Martine
Mary .... Sept. 12
Mara, Marea, Mare,
Marella, Mair, Maire,
Marise, Mariel, Marla,
Maret, Marei, Mae, May,
Maraline, Maria, Marie,
Marian, Mariana, Mariane,
Marien, Mari, Mariella,
Marintha, Marion, Marionette,
Marja, Marsia, Marya,
Marusche, Mascha, Maureen,
Maribel, Marilla, Marilyn,
Mayme, Mollie, Molly
Matilda .... March 14
Machtilde, Mathilde,
Matilde
Matutina .... March 27
Maude .... July 22
Maud, Maudlin
Maura .... Nov. 30
Maure
Mauritia .... Sept. 22
Maxentia .... Nov. 20
Maxima .... April 8
Maximilla .... Feb. 19
Maxine (Maximillian) .... Oct. 12
Mayra .... July 28

Mazota .... Dec. 23
Melania .... Dec. 31
Melanie, Melani, Melany
Melinda (Ermelinda) .... Oct. 29
Mercedes .... Sept. 24
*In honor of Our Lady
of Mercy*
Merced, Mercy, Merry
Merita .... Sept. 22
Messina .... April 19
Michele (Michael) .... Sept. 29
Michelle, Michon, Miguela,
Michaela
Mildred .... July 13
Millie, Milly
Milissa .... March 16
Milice
Mimi (Wilhelmina) ...... March 24
Minna
Mina (Wilhelmina) .... June 25
Minette
Minerva .... Oct. 25
Miriam (Mary) .... Sept. 12
Mitrina .... Aug. 8
Modesta .... Nov. 4
Modesty
Modwenna .... July 5
Moira (Myron) .... Aug. 8
Monessa .... Sept. 4
Monica .... May 4
Mona, Monique
Monice .... April 16
Monna .... Nov. 26
Montana .... May 25
Murenna .... May 26
Muriel (Myron) .... Aug. 8
Mergl, Meriel, Myra
Murina .... May 27
Myra (Myron) .... Aug. 8
Mira, Mirilla, Myrilla
Myrtle (Murial) .... Aug. 8

— N —

Nabara	Oct.	18
Nadine (Hope)	Aug.	1
Nada		
Nana	Nov.	22
Nancy (Anne)	July	26
Nanette, Nanon, Nanna, Nanelia		
Naomi		
Narcissa	March	18
Natalie	July	27
Natalia, Natasha, Natica		
Nathania (Nathaniel)	Aug.	24
Nell (Cornelia)	March	31
Neala, Nelia, Nella, Nelle, Nellis, Nelly, Nelena		
Nessa	July	10
Nessia		
Neysa (Agnes)	Jan.	21
Nice	April	16
Nicea	Aug.	29
Niceta	July	24
Nicolette (Nicholas)	Dec.	6
Nichola, Nicolina		
Nina (Anne)	July	26
Ninetta, Ninon, Nanon		
Nirilla	May	21
Nita (Joan)	May	30
Noel	Dec.	25

Nativity of Our Lord
Noella, Nielle

Nona	Oct.	31
Nonna	Aug.	5
Norah (Honora)	April	12
Nora, Noreen, Norena, Norine		
Norma	Aug.	5
Norrice	Aug.	25
Novella	April	12
Nunciata	March	25

Feast of the Annunciation
Annunciata

Nympha	Nov.	10

— O —

Octavia	April	15
Odella	Feb.	12
Odilia	Dec.	4
Odile, Adilia		
Ola (Olaf)	July	29
Olga	July	11
Helga		
Olive	June	10
Oliva		
Olivia	June	10
Olympia	Dec.	17
Onesta (Honesta)	Oct.	18
Onora (Honora)	April	12
Oona (Winifred)	Nov.	3
Oranda	Sept.	15
Orlanda (Orlando)	May	20
Othilia	Dec.	13
Ottilia		

— P —

Pacifica	March	24
Pamela (Helen)	Aug.	18
Pandonia	Aug.	26
Paris	Aug.	5
Patience	May	1
Patricia	Aug.	25
Patrice		
Paula	Jan.	26
Pala, Poila, Paule, Paulina, Pauline, Paulette, Paulita		
Pearl (Margaret)	June	10
Pelagia	Oct.	8
Penelope (Irene)	Oct.	20
Persia	Feb.	8
Petrine (Peter)	June	29
Petrina		
Petronilla	May	31
Perette, Pernell, Petrina		
Phara	Dec.	7
Philea	Nov.	17

Philene (Philo) .... April 25
Philippa .... May 1
   Philippina, Pippa
Philomena .... Aug. 11
   Filomena
Phoebe .... Sept. 3
   Phebe
Pierrette (Peter) .... June 29
Placida .... Oct. 11
Polly (Molly-Margaret) ....June 10
Polonia (Appolonia) .... Feb. 9
Pontiana .... Feb. 27
Prima .... Feb. 9
Primeva .... Feb. 11
Primitiva .... Feb. 24
Principia .... May 11
Priscilla .... July 8
   Pricilla
Probata .... May 10
Prosperia .... June 25
   Prospera
Prudence .... May 19
   Prudentia, Prue
Purcheria .... Sept. 10
Pura .... Feb. 2

From the Feast of the
Purification of the
Blessed Mother

— Q —

Quartilla .... March 19
Quieta .... Nov. 28
Quinta .... Feb. 8
   Quintina
Quintilla .... March 19
Quirilla .... May 15
Quiteria .... June 4

— R —

Rachel .... Sept. 2
   Rachela, Rachele, Rachelle

Radiana .... Aug. 13
Ragnild .... July 28
Raingarda .... Jan. 26
Rainalda .... July 16
Raissa .... Sept. 5
Ramona (Raymond) .... Jan. 23
Ravenna .... July 23
Raphaela .... Oct. 24
   Rafaela
Raymonda .... Jan. 23
Rebecca
   Reba
Regina .... Sept. 7
   Regia, Reine, Reinette,
   Reina, Reyne
Renata .... March 16
   Renee, Rena
Renelda .... March 22
Reyne .... Sept. 7
Richarda .... April 3
Richelia .... Feb. 1
   Richella
Rita .... May 22
   Reta
Ritza .... Aug. 30
Roberta .... May 13
   Robina, Robenetta,
   Robenette, Robinia
Roderica .... March 13
Rogata .... May 31
Rolanda .... Sept. 15
Rolenda .... May 13
   Rollande, Rollende
Roma .... Jan. 21
Romana .... April 6
   Romaine, Romayne
Romula .... July 23
Ronalda .... Aug. 20
Rosamond .... April 3
Roseline .... Jan. 17
Rosena .... March 17
Rosanne (Rose-Anne) .... July 26

Rosceline .... June 11
   Rosseline
Rose .... Aug. 30
   Rosabel, Rosabelle, Rosalba
   Rosalia, Rosalie, Rosalind,
   Rosalinde, Rosaleen, Rosaline,
   Roseta, Rosetta, Rosette,
   Rosina, Rosita, Rosalyn,
   Rosamond, Rosamund, Roanna,
   Rosel, Roselle, Rosemare,
   Rosetta, Rosina, Rosamary
Roseria .... Oct. 7
   Feast of Our Lady of
     The Rosary
Roxanna .... May 22
   Roxanne, Roxane
Ruby (Robert) .... May 13
   Rubetta
Rudolpha (Rudolph) .... July 27
   Rudolfa
Ruth .... Sept. 1

— S —

Sabela .... Dec. 18
Sabina .... Aug. 29
   Sabine
Sacha (Alexander) .... Feb. 26
Sadie (Sarah) .... Dec. 23
Sallie (Sarah) .... Dec. 23
   Sally
Salome .... June 29
Salomea .... Nov. 17
Samina .... June 2
Samuela .... Aug. 20
Sancha .... March 13
Sancta .... Aug. 16
Sandra (Alexander) .... May 18
Santina .... May 2
Sara .... Dec. 10
Sarah .... Dec. 23
   Sadie, Sarita
Sarapia .... Aug. 29

Sarmatia .... June 2
Sarona .... May 28
Satira .... May 10
Savina .... May 7
Scholastica .... Feb. 10
Sebastiana .... Sept. 16
Secunda .... Jan. 15
   Secundina
Selina (Celestina) .... Sept. 22
   Selena, Selene
Selma (Anselm) .... April 21
Senorina .... April 22
Sentiana .... May 20
Seraphina .... July 29
   Seraphine, Serafine
Serapia .... July 29
Serena .... Aug. 16
Sevilla (Sibylla) .... March 19
Sharon (Rose of Sharon)
   A title of the Blessed Mother
Sheila (Cecilia) .... Nov. 22
   Sheelar, Sheela
Sibylla (Sibyllina) .... March 23
   Sibelle, Sibille, Sibil,
   Sibley, Sibyl, Sibylle,
   Sibylla, Sybilla, Sybila
Sidonia .... Aug. 21
   Sidonie
Silissa .... Oct. 25
Silva .... Dec. 15
Simona .... Feb. 18
   Simonette, Simone
Sirina .... Aug. 26
Sophia .... Sept. 30
   Sofia, Sonia, Sonya, Sophie
Speranza (Hope) .... Aug. 1
Stasia (Anastasia) .... Dec. 25
   Stacie
Stanislawa .... Aug. 15
Stella .... July 10
Stephanie .... Dec. 26
   Stefana, Stefanie

Sue (Susanna) .... Aug. 11
Successa .... March 27
Sunniva .... July 8
   Sunnifa
Susanna .... Aug. 11
   Susan, Susanna, Susanne,
   Susannah, Susie, Suzanna,
   Suzanne, Susy, Suzette
Sylvia .... Nov. 3
   Silvania, Silvia, Silvie,
   Sylwyn
Symphrosia .... July 18
Syria .... June 8

— T —

Talida .... Jan. 5
Tallulah .... June 6
   Tallula
Tama .... Oct. 11
Tamasine (Thomas) .... Dec. 21
Tarasia .... Sept. 3
Tarsitia .... Jan. 15
Tarsilla .... Dec. 24
Tatiana .... Jan. 12
Terentiana .... July 10
   Terentia,
Teresa .... Oct. 15
   Teresina, Terisia, Tess,
   Tessie, Theresa, Therese,
   Theresia, Tressa
Thadine (Thaddeus) .... Oct. 28
Thais .... Oct. 8
Thea .... July 25
Thecla .... Sept. 23
   Tecla, Tekla, Thecle,
   Thekla
Theda (Theodora) .... April 1
Thelma (Anthelmius) .... June 26
Theodora .... April 1
Theodosia .... April 2
Thomasina .... Dec. 21
   Tomasa, Thomasia,
   Thomasine

Tilda (Matilda) .... March 14
   Tillie
Timothea .... Jan. 24
Tina
   Nickname for several names,
   e.g. Ernestine, Christina,
   Martina, etc.
Titiana .... July 17
Toscana .... Dec. 18
   Tosca, Toscaine
Trina (Catherine) .... April 30
   Trine, Trinette
Trixie (Beatrice) .... July 29
   Tryce
Trophe (Eutropia) .... Dec. 14
Trude (Gertrude) .... Nov. 16
   Trudel, Trudy

— U —

Udelina .... Oct. 19
Uganda .... June 3
Ulrica (Ulric) .... July 4
   Ulrika, Ulrique
Una (Winifred) .... Nov. 3
Urania .... May 28
Urbana .... May 17
Ursa .... Oct. 26
Ursula .... Oct. 21
   Ursel, Ursele

— V —

Valdrada .... May 5
Valentia .... June 2
   Valentine
Valeria .... June 5
   Valerie
Valeriana .... Nov. 15
Vanessa (Esther) .... July 1
Vaune .... Nov. 9
Vanora .... Jan. 3
Vaudree .... May 5
Vendreda (Winifred) ...... June 5
Venetia (Beatrice) .... July 29
   Venice

Venisa .... July 12
Vera .... Jan. 24
Verbetta .... Sept. 16
Verdiana .... Feb. 1
Verena .... Sept. 1
Verona .... Aug. 29
Veronica .... July 12
   Verenice, Veron, Venise
Vestina .... July 17
   Vesta
Vevette (Genevieve) .... Jan. 3
Vicentia (Vincent) .... April 5
Victory .... Dec. 23
   Victoria, Victoire
   Victorie
Victorina .... Oct. 18
   Victorine
Vidette (David) .... Dec. 29
   Vida
Vigilia .... June 26
Vincentia .... April 5
Viola .... May 3
   Violante, Violet,
   Violetta, Violette
Virginia
In Honor of The Blessed Virgin
Vitalina .... Feb. 21
Viventia .... March 17
Vivian .... Dec. 2
   Viva, Vivien, Vivienne
Vladislawa (Ladislaus) .. June 27

— W —

Wanda (Wando) .... April 17
Walburga .... Feb. 25
Wilfreda .... Sept. 9
   Wilfrida

Wilhelmina (William) .... June 25
   Willa, Wileen, Willabel,
   Willabelle, Wilhelmine,
   Wilette, Williamina.
   Helmina
Winifred .... Nov. 3
   Winfreda

— X —

Xantippa .... Sept. 23
   Xantippe
Xaverie (Xavier) .... Dec. 3
Xene .... Jan. 24
Xenia .... Sept. 23
   Zenia
Ximena (Simon) .... Oct. 28
Xina (Christina) .... July 24

— Y —

Yoland .... April 23
   Yolaine
Yolanda .... Dec. 28
   Yolande, Yolanthe,
   Yolette
Ysabeau (Isabel) .... July 8
   Ysabel
Ytha (Ita) .... Jan. 15
Yvonne (Ivo) .... May 19
   Yvette

— Z —

Zandra (Alexandra) .... May 18
Zanetta (Joanna) .... May 24
Zara (Sarah) .... Dec. 23
Zelina (Soline) .... Oct. 17
Zenia .... Sept. 23
Zenobia .... Oct. 30
Zita .... April 27
Zoe .... July 5
Zona .... Feb. 9
   Zoa

CHRISTIAN NAMES
BOYS

— A —

Aaron .... July 1
Abban .... Oct. 27
Abel .... Dec. 2
Abraham .... Oct. 9
   Abram
Absolan .... March 2
Achille (Achilles) .... Nov. 7
Achim (Joachim) .... Aug. 16
Achmed .... Dec. 24
Adalbert .... April 23
   Adelbert
Adam .... Dec. 24
Adolph .... June 17
   Adolfo, Adolphe,
   Adolphus, Dolph
Adrian .... Sept. 8
   Hadrian
Adrien .... April 1
Aeneas (Angus) .... March 11
Ailbe .... Sept. 12
Aime .... Sept. 13
Alain .... Oct. 26
Alair (Hilary) .... Jan. 14
Alan .... Oct. 26
Alaric .... Sept. 29
Alban .... June 22
   Albany, Albin
Albert .... Nov. 15
   Albrecht, Alberto,
   Albertino, Elbert
Albian .... June 10
Albin .... March 1
Alcuin .... May 19

Alexander .... Feb. 26
   Alessandro, Alexandre
   Sandor, Sandro, Sanders,
   Sacha
Alexis .... July 17
   Alexian, Alexio, Alexios,
   Aleixo, Alexe, Alessio,
   Alexius
Alfred .... Aug. 15
Alger .... April 11
Allan .... Jan. 12
   Allen
Alleyn .... Feb. 22
Aloysius .... June 21
   Alois, Aloisio, Aloys
Alphonsus .... Aug. 2
   Alfons, Alfonso, Alonso,
   Alphonse, Alphonso
Alvin .... Dec. 7
Alton (Alto) .... Feb. 9
Amadeus .... Jan. 28
Ambrose .... Dec. 7
   Ambrosio, Ambroise,
   Ambrozi, Bruce
Americus (Emmeric) ...... Nov. 4
   Almeric, Americo, Amerigo,
   Amery, Amory
Amos .... March 31
Anastasius .... Dec. 19
Anatole .... July 3
   Anatol
Ancel (Lancelot) .... June 27
Andrew .... Nov. 30
   Anders, Andre, Andrea,
   Andrus, Andres
Angelo .... May 5

Angus .... March 11
Anselm .... April 21
  Ansel, Anselme, Anselmo
Ansgar .... Feb. 3
Anthony .... June 13
  Anton, Antoni, Antonie,
  Antonio
Antony .... Jan. 17
Aquinas .... March 7
  Aquin
Archibald .... March 27
Ardan .... Feb. 11
Aristo .... Dec. 3
Armand .... Jan. 23
Armon .... July 31
Arnold .... March 14
  Arnald, Arnaud, Arne,
  Arno, Arnoldo, Arend,
  Arnoul
Arsene .... July 19
Artemus .... Jan. 24
Arthur .... Dec. 11
  Arturo, Artur
Ashley (Bl. Ralph) ...... April 7
Athanasius .... May 2
Aubert .... Sept. 10
Aubin .... March 1
  Aubert
Aubrey .... Nov. 14
Augustine .... Aug. 28
  Auguste, Augustin,
  Augustino, Austin,
  Austen, Gus
Augustus .... Oct. 7
Aurelian .... July 16
Austell .... June 28
Authbert .... Dec. 13
Authaire .... April 24
Axel (Alexis) .... July 17
Aymar .... July 15
Azarias .... Feb. 3

— B —

Baldwin .... July 15
  Balduin
Baltram .... Jan. 18
Baptist (St. John the) .... June 24
  Baptiste
Bardo .... June 10
Barlow .... Sept. 10
  (Blessed Ambrose)
Barnabas .... June 11
  Barnaby, Barney, Barna
Barnard .... Jan. 23
Barr (Finnbar) .... Sept. 25
Barrion (Finnbar) .... Sept. 25
Barry (Finnbar) .... Sept. 25
Batholomew .... Aug. 24
  Bart, Bartek, Bartel,
  Barthole, Bathleme,
  Bartlett, Bartley, Barton,
  Bertel, Barto, Bartolomeo
Basil .... June 14
  Basile, Basine, Vasili
Bastien (Sebastian) .... Jan. 20
Becket (St. Thomas) .... Dec. 29
Bede .... May 27
Beltram .... March 1
Benedict .... March 21
  Benedic, Bendek, Benedik,
  Benedicto, Benito, Bennett,
  Benedetto
Benjamin .... March 21
Benno .... June 16
Berchmans .... Aug. 13
Bernard .... Aug. 20
  Barend, Barnaro, Berend,
  Bernal, Bernardino,
  Bernardo, Bernhard, Berns,
  Burnet
Bertold .... Oct. 21
Bertran .... Jan. 24

Bertrand .... June 6
Bertram, Berton, Bert
Beverley (John B.) .... May 7
Blaise (Blase) .... Feb. 3
Blaze
Blandin .... May 1
Blane .... Aug. 10
Blaine
Boetius .... Oct. 23
Bonaventure .... July 14
Boniface .... June 5
Bonifaze
Boris .... July 24
Borromeo (St. Charles) .... Nov. 4
Boswell (Boisil) .... July 7
Brandan .... Oct. 20
Brannock .... Jan. 7
Brendan .... May 16
Brennan .... May 6
Brian .... March 22
Brien, Bryan
Briant (Bl. Alex) .... Dec. 1
Brice .... Nov. 13
Brinstan .... Nov. 4
Bristan
Brittan .... May 19
Brogan .... Sept. 17
Bruce (Ambrose) .... Dec. 7
Bruno .... Oct. 6
Burton (Bertinus) .... Sept. 5
Byron (Birinus) .... Dec. 3

— C —

Cadoc .... Jan. 24
Cadwallader .... Nov. 12
Caesar .... Aug. 27
Cesar
Cahil (Charles) .... Nov. 4
Caius .... April 22
Cajetan .... Aug. 7
Caleb .... Oct. 27
Calixtus .... Oct. 14

Callen .... Nov. 28
Camillus .... July 18
Camille, Comillo
Campion (Bl. Edmund) .... Dec. 1
Cantius .... May 31
Canute .... Jan. 7
Knute, Kanut, Canut, Cnud
Carter (Carterius) .... Nov. 2
Cary .... Jan. 3
Casimir .... March 4
Casmir, Kasmir
Casper .... Jan. 28
Caspar
Cass .... Aug. 13
Cato .... Dec. 28
Cecil .... Feb. 1
Celestine .... July 27
Chad .... March 2
Charles .... Nov. 4
Cahil, Carel, Carol, Carl,
Carlo, Carlos, Charlet,
Charlot, Karl, Karel,
Karol, Carlton
Chester (Ceslaus) .... July 17
Chris (Christian) .... March 18
Christopher .... July 25
Christophe, Christof
Chrysostom .... Jan. 27
Ciro (Cyriac) .... Aug. 8
Clair (Clarus) .... Nov. 4
Clarence .... April 25
Claret (Bl. Anthony) .... Oct. 24
Claud .... June 6
Claude, Claudio
Claus (Nicholas) .... Dec. 6
Clement .... Nov. 23
Clem, Clemence, Clemento,
Clemente
Clovis (Louis) .... Aug. 25
Colan .... May 21
Colin (Nicholas) .... Dec. 6
Colman .... Nov. 24

Coleman (Bl. Edward) .... Dec. 1
Colum .... Sept. 22
Columbanus .... Nov. 21
Conald .... Sept. 24
Conan .... March - 8
Conon .... Feb. 26
Conrad .... Feb. 19
   Court
Constantine .... July 27
   Kurt, Curt
Consul .... July 7
Cormac .... Sept. 14
Cornelius .... Sept. 16
   Corney, Neal, Nelson,
   Corneille
Cosmo .... Sept. 27
   Cosmas
Credan .... Aug. 19
Crescent (Cresentius) .... April 19
Cronan .... April 28
Cullan .... May 21
Cuthbert .... March 20
Cyriacus .... Aug. 8
Cyprian .... Sept. 16
   Cyprien
Cyr .... June 16
   Cyrano, Cyran, Cyrin
Cyril .... July 7
   Cyrill, Cyrille, Cirilo
Cyrus .... Jan. 31

—D —

Damian .... April 12
   Damien, Damio
Daniel .... July 21
   Danil, Dannel, Danny
Darius .... Dec. 19
David .... Dec. 29
   Dawid, Dave, Davie
Declan .... July 24
Dedric (Theodoric) .... July 1
Damarius .... Sept. 30

Dennis .... Oct. 9
   Denez, Denis, Dennet,
   Denys, Dinis
Deodatus .... April 24
Dermit .... March 2
Dermot .... Jan. 18
Desire (Desiderius) .... Sept. 16
Devereaux .... Nov. 14
   Devereau
Dewey (David) .... March 1
Dexter .... May 7
Diago (James) .... July 25
   Diego
Dietrich (Theobald) .... June 30
Dion .... July 6
Dionysius .... Oct. 9
Dismas .... March 25
Dmitri (Demetrius) .... Oct. 8
   Dimitar
Dominic .... Aug. 4
   Diminick, Domingo,
   Domenico
Donald .... July 15
   Don, Donnie
Donan .... April 17
Donard .... March 24
Donat .... March 24
Donatus .... Aug. 7
Dreux .... April 16
Duane .... Feb. 11
Dunstan .... May 19
Durdan .... Sept. 5
Durban (Urban) .... May 25
   Durbin
Dustan .... July 11

— E —

Eagan .... May 31
Eamon (Edmund) .... Nov. 16
Earl (Herluin) .... Aug. 26
Edbert .... May 6
Edfrid .... Oct. 26

Edgar .... July 8
Edmund .... Nov. 16
   Edmond, Tedmund
Ednyfed .... May 21
Edwald .... March 23
Edward .... Oct. 13
   Edsel, Edson, Ned, Eduard,
   Edvard, Ward
Edwin .... Oct. 12
Egbert .... April 24
Eldred .... March 13
Elgar .... June 14
Elias .... July 20
   Ellis, Eliot, Elliott
Eligius .... Dec. 1
Elmer .... Aug. 28
Elmo .... June 2
Elvis .... Feb. 22
Elwin .... Feb. 22
Emery .... Nov. 4
Emil .... Feb. 1
   Emile
Emilian .... Nov. 12
Emmanuel .... July 10
   Emanuel, Emminuel
Emmeric .... Nov. 4
   Americo, Americus, Amery,
   Emery, Emory
Enoch .... March 26
Enos .... May 1
Enrico (Henry) .... July 15
Ephrem .... June 18
Erasmus .... June 2
Eric .... May 18
   Erich, Erick, Erik
Ermin .... April 25
Ernest .... Nov. 7
   Ernesto, Ernst, Erneste
Ervan (Ervin) .... May 29
Esdras .... July 13
Esme (Osmund) .... Dec. 4

Esteban (Stephan) .... Dec. 26
   Etienne
Ethelbert .... Feb. 24
Ethian (Ethern) .... May 27
Eugene .... June 2
   Eugen, Eugenio, Gene
Eustace .... Sept. 20
   Eustis
Evan .... Aug. 18
Evelyn .... Dec. 19
Ewald .... Oct. 3
Ezechiel .... April 10
Ezra .... July 13

— F —

Fabian .... Jan. 20
   Fabien
Falco .... Feb. 20
Farrel (Fergus) .... Nov. 18
Felician .... Jan. 24
Felix .... May 30
   Felice
Felipe (Phillip) .... May 1
Felton (Bl. John) .... Aug. 8
Ferdinand .... May 20
   Fernando, Ferrante, Ferd,
   Ferde
Fergus .... March 29
Fiacre .... Aug. 30
Filbert (Philbert) .... Aug. 20
Finbarr .... Sept. 25
Fingar .... Dec. 14
Finian .... Oct. 21
Flavian .... Feb. 18
Flobert .... Dec. 31
Florens .... Dec. 29
Florian .... May 4
Floyd (Florentius) .... June 9
Forde .... May 28
Fortis .... May 9
Foster (Vedast) .... Feb. 6

Francis .... Oct.   4
   Fanchon, Franc, Francisco,
   Franco, Francois, Franek,
   Frank, Pancho, Franz,
   Franklin
Frederick .... July 18
   Fred, Frederic,
   Frederico, Fritz
Freeman (Bl. William) ....Aug. 13
Fulk .... Oct. 26

— G —

Gabriel .... March 24
   Gabrielo, Gavril
Galen .... June 22
Gall .... Oct. 16
Gallan .... Dec.   7
Garcia .... Feb.   5
Gardiner (Bl. George)....March   7
Garibaldi .... Jan.   8
Garnier .... July 19
Garret (Gerald) .... Oct. 13
   Garrett
Gaspar .... Dec. 28
Gaston .... Feb.   6
Gatian .... Dec. 18
Gaudens .... Jan. 22
Gautier .... April   9
Gedeon .... Sept.   1
   Gideon
Gelasius .... Nov. 21
Gentian .... Dec. 11
Geoffrey (Godfrey) .... Nov.   8
George .... April 23
   Georg, Georgt, Giorgio,
   Gorg, Joris, Jurgen
Gerald .... Oct. 13
   Garcia, Gerry, Girald
   Garret, Garrett, Jarett
Gerard .... Oct. 16
   Geraud, Gerhard, Giraud
Gerold .... April 19

Geronimo (Jerome) .... Sept. 30
Gervase .... June 19
Gery (Gaudric) .... Aug. 11
Gilbert .... Feb.   4
   Gilberto, Gisbert
Gildas .... Jan. 29
Giles .... Sept.   1
   Gilles, Gillet, Gil
Giotto (Godfrey) .... Nov.   8
Giovanni (John) .... Dec. 27
Girard .... Dec. 29
Giuseppe (Joseph) .... March 19
Goddard .... May   4
   Godard
Godfrey .... Nov.   8
   Geoffrey, Jeffrey, Joffre
Godwin .... Oct. 28
   Goodwin
Gonzaga .... June 21
Gordian .... Sept. 17
   Gordien
Gordius .... Jan.   3
   Gordon
Gorman .... Aug. 28
Gottfried (Godfrey) .... Nov. 28
Gottschalk .... June   7
Gratian .... Dec. 18
Gregory .... March 12
   Gregor, Gregus, Gregorio
   Gregoire, Gregg
Griffith .... July   1
Guarian .... July 27
Guido .... Sept. 12
Gunther .... Sept.   9
Gustave (Augustus) .... Oct.   7
Guy .... Sept. 12
   Guidon, Guyon

— H —

Habert .... Dec. 19
Hadrian (Adrian) .... Sept.   8
Happy (Felix) .... May 30

Harding (Bl. Stephen) ....April 17
Harold .... March 25
Harry (Henry) .... July 15
Hart (Bl. William) ...... March 13
Harvey .... Feb. 17
Harward .... Sept. 16
  Harwarld
Henry .... July 15
  Hawkins, Henning, Hendrik,
  Henriot, Henryk, Heinrich,
  Hal, Enrico, Enzio
Herbert .... March 20
Herman .... April 7
Hermangild .... April 13
Hermes .... Jan. 4
Hero .... June 28
Hilary .... Jan. 14
  Alair, Hilaire, Hilario
Hildebrand .... May 25
Hobart (Hubert) .... Nov. 3
Hodge (Robert) .... May 13
Howard (Bl. William) .... Dec. 29
Howell (Hywell) .... Jan. 6
Hubert .... Nov. 3
  Hubbard
Hudson (Bl. James) ...... Nov. 28
Hugh .... April 29
  Hugo, Hughes
Humbert .... March 4
Humphrey .... March 8
  Humphry
Hutchin (Hugh) .... April 29
Hyacinth .... Aug. 16
  Hyacinthe

— I —

Iago (James) .... July 25
Ian (John) .... Dec. 27
Ignatius .... July 31
  Ignace, Ignacy, Ignazio
Igor .... June 5
Imbert .... Sept. 6

Immanuel .... July 10
Innocent .... July 28
Irvin (Urban) .... May 25
  Irving
Isaac .... Sept. 9
Isaias .... July 5
Isidore .... April 4
  Isidro
Israel .... Dec. 22
Ivan .... June 24
Ives .... April 24
Ivo .... May 19
  Ivar

— J —

Jacinte (Hyacinth) .... Aug. 16
Jacob .... Dec. 19
James .... July 25
  Jacques, Jacob, Jago,
  Jaime, Jamek, Jamnik,
  Jayme, Shamus
Januarius .... Sept. 19
Jared .... March 1
Jareth .... Oct. 27
Jarett (Gerald) .... Oct. 13
Jarlath .... Feb. 11
Jarmin .... Feb. 23
Jason .... July 12
Jasper (Caspar) .... Dec. 28
Jeffry (Godfrey) .... Nov. 8
Jeremias .... May 1
  Jeremy
Jerome .... Sept. 30
  Jeronimo, Geromino
Jesse .... Dec. 29
Jesus

*The name of Our Blessed Lord
and Savior. Many peoples, out
of reverence, do not use it as a
given name; others, notably the
Spanish, taking a different view,
frequently give it in Baptism.*

Joachim .... Aug. 16
  Joaquin
Jocelyn .... March 17
  Josselin
Job .... May 10
Joel .... July 13
John .... Dec. 27
  Hansel, Ian, Jan, Johan,
  Johann, Juan, Shawn,
  Giovanni, Janek
Jonas .... Sept. 21
Jordan .... Feb. 15
Joris (George) .... April 23
Joseph .... March 19
  Jose, Josef, Jozef,
  Guiseppe
Josue .... Sept. 1
Jovian .... June 1
Joyce .... Dec. 13
Jude .... Oct. 28
Julian .... March 8
  Julien
Julius .... April 12
  Jules
Junius .... May 17
Jurgen (George) .... April 23
Justin .... April 14
Justus .... Nov. 10

— K —

Kanut (Canute) .... Jan. 7
Karl (Charles) .... Nov. 4
  Karol, Karel
Kasimir (Casimir) .... March 4
Kaspar (Caspar) .... Dec. 28
  Kasper, Kass
Kelan (Callen) .... Nov. 28
Kellen .... March 26
Kellog .... April 1
Kemble (Bl. John) .... Aug. 22
Kenelm .... July 17
Kennan .... Feb. 25

Kenan
Kenneth .... Oct. 11
  Kenny, Kenzie
Kent (Kentigern) .... Jan. 14
Kernan .... Nov. 5
Kerstan (Christian) ...... April 18
Kevin (Keevin) .... June 3
Kieran .... Sept. 9
Kilian .... July 8
Killian .... Nov. 13
Kim Korean Martyrs
Klas (Nicholas) .... Dec. 6
  Klaas, Klaus
Knute .... Jan. 7
Konrad .... Feb. 19
Kristopher .... July 25
Kurt (Constantine) .... July 27

— L —

Lacy (Bl. William) .... Aug. 22
Ladislaus .... June 27
  Ladislas, Lancelot
Lambert .... Sept. 17
  Lamberto, Lambrecht
Lancelot .... June 27
  Ancel, Lance
Landert .... Sept. 17
Landry .... April 17
Lanfranc .... June 23
Laurus .... Sept. 30
Lawrence .... Aug. 10
  Lars, Larkin, Larse,
  Lauren, Lauritz, Loren,
  Lorenz, Lorenzo, Lorin,
  Lorus, Lawrie
Lazarus .... Dec. 17
  Lazar, Lazare, Lazaro
Leander .... Feb. 27
Leo .... April 11
  Leon, Lionel, Lee
Leonard .... Nov. 26
  Leonardo, Lenny

Leopold .... Nov. 15
Lester (Sylvester) .... Dec. 31
Levi .... Dec. 22
Libertus .... Dec. 20
Liguori (St. Alphonsus)....Aug. 2
Linus .... Sept. 25
Llewelyn .... April 7
  Llywelen
Lochen .... June 12
Lockwood (Bl. John)......April 13
Longinus .... March 15
Loran .... Aug. 30
Lothaire .... June 14
Lothar .... June 14
Louis .... Aug. 25
  Clovis, Lewis, Ludwig,
  Loiz, Luigi, Luis
Loyola (St. Ignatius) ...... July 31
  Lyle
Lucas .... June 27
Lucian .... Jan. 7
  Lucien
Lucius .... March 4
Ludwig .... Aug. 25
Luke .... Oct. 18
  Lucas, Lukas
Luxor .... Aug. 21

— M —

Macarius .... Jan. 2
  Macaire
Mace (Matthew) .... Sept. 21
Macniss .... Sept. 3
Macson (Maximus) .... Aug. 13
Magnus .... Nov. 5
Mainard .... Jan. 21
Maine .... June 21
Major .... May 10
Malachy .... Nov. 3
  Loughlan
Malcolm .... June 3
Manasses .... Nov. 5

Manfred .... Jan. 28
Manuel .... July 10
Marcellus .... Jan. 16
  Marcel
Marcian .... June 14
  Marcien
Maris .... April 26
Mark .... April 25
  Marc, Marco, Mario
Marmaduke .... Nov. 26
Marnack .... March 1
Marne .... Sept. 2
Marshall .... June 30
Marten .... Aug. 18
Martial .... June 30
Martian .... June 14
Martin .... Nov. 11
  Marti, Martino, Marten,
  Martil, Mertin, Marvin
Matthew .... Sept. 21
  Mathew, Mathies,
  Mathieu, Matt
Matthias .... Feb. 24
  Mathias
Maur .... Jan 15
Maurice .... Jan. 15
  Mauras, Mauritz, Maury,
  Moris, Moritz, Morris
Maximain .... June 9
Maximilian .... Oct. 12
Maximus .... Jan. 15
Maynard .... May 9
Medard .... June 8
Meinrad .... Jan. 21
Mel .... Feb. 6
Melchior .... Jan. 6
Meldan .... Feb. 7
Melvin .... July 17
Merald .... Feb. 23
Merchard .... Aug. 24
Mercury (Mercurius) ......Nov. 25
Meredith (Murtaugh) ......Aug. 13

Methodius	July 7	Noah	May 2
Michael	Sept. 29	Noe	
Micha, Michal, Michaud,		Noel	Dec. 25
Michel, Michele, Mickel,		Norbert	June 6
Miguel, Mikel, Misha,			
Mitchell			

— O —

Miles	April 30	Obert	Dec. 11
Myles		Octavius	Nov. 20
Milo	Feb. 23	Odemar	May 7
Miron	Aug. 8	Odilo	Jan. 1
Monald	March 15	Odilon	Oct. 28
Monford	July 2	Odo	Nov. 18
Moran	Oct. 22	Odoric	Feb. 3
Morand	June 3	Olaf	July 30
More (St. Thomas)	July 9	Oleg	Sept. 20
Morgan	May 15	Olier (Oliver)	July 11
Mortimer	Aug. 12	Oliver	July 11
Moses	Sept. 4	Olivier	
Murdoch	Sept. 2	Omer	Sept. 9
Myles	April 30	Oran	Oct. 27
Myron	Aug. 8	Odran	
		Orestes	Dec. 13

— N —

		Orlando	May 20
Nacaro	Jan. 8	Orland	
Naldo (Ronald)	Aug. 20	Ormond	Jan. 23
Napoleon	Aug. 15	Osmund	Dec. 4
Napper (Bl. George)	Nov. 9	Orson	April 13
Narcissus	March 18	Oscar	Feb. 3
Nathan	Dec. 29	Oskar	
Nathaniel	Aug. 24	Osmond	Dec. 4
Neal (Cornelius)	Sept. 16	Oswald	Aug. 5
Neil, Nelson		Othmar	Nov. 16
Neon	Dec. 2	Otho	Jan. 16
Nepomucene (St. John)	May 16	Otto	July 2
Nestor	Feb. 26	Eudus, Othello	
Neville (Alban)	June 22	Owen	March 3
Nevin			

— P —

Nicholas	Dec. 6		
Claus, Colin, Klaas, Klas,		Pancratius	March 12
Klaus, Niel, Nico		Pantaleon	July 27
Nicodemus	Aug. 3	Paris	Aug. 5
Niles (Nicholas)	Dec. 6		

Paschal	May 17	Rainer	Dec. 30
Pascal, Pascoe, Pasquale, Pasinek		Rainier	
Patrician	Oct. 10	Ralph	July 7
Patrick	March 17	Randal, Randall, Randolph,	
Paton, Patrig, Patrizio, Payton, Peyton		Randolf, Raoul, Rolf, Rollo, Roul, Rodolfo	
Paul	June 29	Rambert	June 13
Pablo, Paley, Paolo,		Raphael	Oct. 24
Paulot, Paulus, Pavel, Pawel		Raymond	Jan. 23
Payne (Bl. John)	April 2	Raimundo, Ramon	
Pepin	Feb. 21	Raynald	Aug. 18
Percy	Nov. 14	Rayner	Feb. 22
Percival		Raynier	
Peregrine	May 1	Reginald	April 9
Peter	June 29	Reynold, Reinald,	
Pearce, Peder, Pedro,		Reynaud, Reynalt	
Peirce, Pierce, Peire, Pierot,		Regius	June 18
Perrin, Perry, Pierson		Regnier	Feb. 22
Philibert	Aug. 20	Reinhard	March 7
Philip	May 1	Reinhold (Reginald)	Sept. 17
Filipe, Fillipo, Lipo		Reinold	Jan. 7
Philo	April 25	Rembert	Feb. 4
Phineas	Aug. 12	Remi	Oct. 1
Pierson (Bl. Walter)	May 4	Remy	
Pius	May 5	Rene	Feb. 22
Placid	Oct. 5	Renier, Reno	
Plato	April 4	Rex	April 9
Plunket (Bl. Oliver)	July 11	Rhodian	March 20
Polycarp	Jan. 26	Rich (Bl. Edmund)	Nov. 16
Pompey	Dec. 14	Richard	April 3
Porphyry	Feb. 26	Ricardo, Ritch, Ritchie,	
Porres (Bl. Martin)	Nov. 5	Rykart	
Princeps	Aug. 22	Robert	May 13
Prosper	July 25	Robard, Roberto, Robin,	
		Hodge	
— Q —		Roch	Aug. 16
Quartan	Sept. 3	Rock, Roque	
Quentin	Oct. 31	Rochester (Bl. John)	May 4
Quintian	Nov. 13	Rodan	April 15
Quirin	June 4	Roderic	May 13
— R —		Roderick, Roderigo	
Rainald	Aug. 18	Royce, Ruy	

Rodion .... April 8
Rodolf .... July 27
Roger .... Aug. 16
   Rogerio, Rogero, Rodger,
   Rutger, Rory
Roland .... Nov. 15
   Rolando, Rowland
Romain .... Feb. 28
   Roman
Romeo .... March 4
Ronald .... Aug. 20
Ronan .... June 1
Rorie (Roger) .... Aug. 16
   Rory
Rothard .... Oct. 14
Roy (Rufus) .... Nov. 21
Ruben .... Aug. 4
Rubert .... May 15
Rudolph .... July 27
   Rudolf, Rudolphe, Rolf,
   Rolph, Rollin, Rollo
Rufus .... Nov. 21
Rupert .... March 27
   Ruprecht
Rurik .... May 13
Rutger (Roger) .... Aug. 16
Ruy (Roderic) .... March 13

— S —

Sacha (Alexander) .... Feb. 26
   Sanders, Sandor, Sandro,
   Sandy
Salvator .... March 18
Sampson .... July 28
   Samson
Samuel .... Aug. 20
   Samuele
Sancho (Sanctus) .... June 2
   Sanctos
Sandor (Alexander) .... Feb. 26
   Sandro
Santiago (St. James) ...... July 25

Saul .... Feb. 16
Sebastian .... Jan. 20
Senator .... Sept. 26
Seran .... March 6
Sergius .... Sept. 8
   Serge, Sergio
Seth .... March 1
Severin .... Oct. 23
Seward (Siviard) .... March 1
Shamus (James) .... July 25
Shawn (John) .... Dec. 27
Sheil .... Feb. 12
Sherwin (Bl. Ralph) .... Dec. 1
Sherwood (Bl. Thomas) March 7
Sibold .... Oct. 26
Sidney .... Sept. 19
Sigefried .... Feb. 15
   Sigefrid
Sigfrid .... Feb. 15
   Siward
Sigismund .... May 1
   Sigmund
Silas .... July 13
Silvester .... Dec. 31
Silvio .... May 31
   Sylvio
Simeon .... Feb. 18
Simon .... Oct. 28
   Simone
Sinclair (St. Clair) .... Nov. 4
Sirmion .... April 9
Sixtus .... April 6
Slade (Bl. Thomas) .... Oct. 30
Solomon .... March 13
Spur .... Jan. 16
Stanislaus .... Aug. 15
   Stanislao, Stanko, Stanley
Stephen .... Dec. 26
   Stephan, Stefano, Stepka,
   Steven, Esteban
Sulpice .... Jan. 17
Swithin .... July 2

Sydney .... Dec. 10
Sylvester .... Dec. 31

— T —

Tancred .... April 9
Tarcissus .... Aug. 15
Tatian .... Aug. 24
Tedmund (Edmund) .... Nov. 16
Tegan .... Sept. 9
Terrence .... Aug. 29
   Terence, Terry
Thaddeus .... Oct. 28
Theodore .... Nov. 9
   Theodor, Fedor
Theodoric .... July 1
   Theodric, Thierry
Thibaud .... June 30
Thomas .... Dec. 21
   Tomas, Tomasso, Tomaz
Thurstan .... March 31
Timothy .... Jan. 24
Titian .... Jan. 16
Titus .... Feb. 6
   Tito
Tobias .... Nov. 2
Toussaint (All Saints) .... Nov. 1
   Toussant
Trajan .... Dec. 23
Tybalt .... June 30

— U —

Ugo (Hugh) .... April 29
Ulric .... July 4
Ulmer .... July 20
Urban .... May 25
Ursino .... Nov. 9
Ursus .... April 13

— V —

Valentine .... Feb. 14
Valerius .... Jan. 29

Valery .... April 1
Valerian .... Nov. 27
Valter (Walter) .... June 4
Vardan .... Aug. 7
Vedast .... Feb. 6
Vernon (Berno) .... Jan. 13
Viator .... Oct. 21
Victor .... July 28
Vigor .... Nov. 1
Vinard .... Oct. 11
Vincent .... July 19
   Vicente, Vincens, Vincenti,
   Vance
Virgil .... Nov. 27
Vitus .... June 15
Vivian .... Aug. 28
   Vivien
Vladimar .... July 15

— W —

Walter .... June 4
   Walther, Walthier, Water,
   Wolter
Ward (Bl. William) .... July 26
Warren .... Feb. 6
Webster (Bl. Augustine)....Feb. 6
Wenceslaus .... Sept. 28
   Wenzel, Wenceslas
Wendelyn .... Oct. 21
   Wendel, Wendell
Werner .... April 19
Whiting (Bl. Richard) .... Nov. 14
Wilbert .... Sept. 11
   Wilbur
Wilfred .... April 24
   Wilfrid
William .... June 25
   Wilhelm, Guillaume,
   Quillen, Willin
Winfred .... Nov. 3
   Winfrid

Wolfgang .... Feb. 1
   Wolf
Wright (Bl. Peter) .... May 19
Wulfram .... March 20

— X —

Xavier (St. Francis) .... Dec. 3
   Xaver, Xavery, Savero
Ximen (Simon) .... Oct. 28

— Y —

Yago (James) .... July 25
   Iago
Yves .... May 19
   Yvo

— Z —

Zachary .... Nov. 5
   Zacharius
Zeno .... April 12

PATRON SAINTS AND
THEIR FEAST DAYS

Long established custom and devotion have established these
saints as patrons. In a few instances the designations
have been made by the Holy See.

ACTORS —
St. Genesius ....Aug. 25

ALTAR BOYS —
St. John Berchmans ....Aug. 13

ARCHITECTS —
St. Thomas the Apostle....Dec. 21

ARTILLERYMEN —
St. Barbara ....Dec. 4

ARTISTS —
St. Luke ....Oct. 18

ASTRONOMERS —
St. Dominic ....Aug. 4

ATHLETES —
St. Sebastian ....Jan. 20

AUTHORS —
St. Francis de Sales ....Jan. 29

AUTOMOBILISTS —
St. Christopher ....July 25

AVIATORS —
Our Lady of Loretto ....Dec. 10

BAKERS —
St. Elizabeth of Hungary Nov. 19

BANK WORKERS —
St. Matthew ....Sept. 21

BARBERS —
SS. Cosmas & Damian......Sept. 27

BARREN WOMEN —
St. Anthony of Padua......June 13

BEGGARS —
St. Alexius ....July 17

BLACKSMITHS —
St. Dunstan ....May 19

BLIND —
St. Raphael ....Oct. 24

BOOK INDUSTRY WORKERS—
BOOKMAKERS —
St. Peter Celestine ....May 19

BOOKSELLERS —
St. John of God ....March 8

BOY SCOUTS —
St. George ....April 23

BREWERS —
St. Nicholas ....Dec. 6

BRICKLAYERS —
St. Stephen ....Dec. 26

BRUSH-MAKERS —
St. Anthony, Ab. ....Jan. 17

BUILDING INDUSTRY
WORKERS —
St. Vincent Ferrer ....April 5

BUS DRIVERS —
St. Christopher ....July 25

BUTCHERS —
St. Hadrian ....Sept. 8

CAB DRIVERS —
St. Fiacre ....Aug. 30

CABINET MAKERS —
St. Anne ....July 26

CARPENTERS —
St. Joseph ....March 19

CATHOLIC ACTION —
St. Francis of Assisi ....Oct. 4

CEMETERIES &
CEMETERY WORKERS —
St. Anthony, Ab. ....Jan. 17

CHARITABLE SOCIETIES —
St. Vincent de Paul ....July 19

CHEMICAL INDUSTRY
WORKERS —
SS. Cosmas & Damian....Sept. 27

CLOTHING INDUSTRY
  WORKERS,
  WEAVERS —
  St. Paul the Hermit ....Jan. 15

  DYERS —
  SS. Maurice & Lydia ....Aug. 3

COMEDIANS —
  St. Vitus ....June 15

CONDEMNED TO DEATH —
  St. Dismas ....March 25

CONFESSORS —
  St. John Nepomucene ....May 16

COOKS —
  St. Martha ....July 29

COOPERS —
  St. Nicholas ....Dec. 6

DEAF —
  St. Frances de Sales ....Jan. 29

DENTISTS —
  St. Apollonia ....Feb. 9

DESPERATE SITUATIONS —
  St. Jude Thaddeus ....Oct. 28

DIOCESAN PRIESTS —
  St. Jean - Baptiste
  Vianney .... Aug. 9

DOCTORS —
  St. Luke ....Oct. 18

DOMESTIC ANIMALS —
  St. Anthony, Abbott ....Jan. 17

DRUGGISTS —
  SS. Cosmas & Damian ....Sept. 27

ENGINEERS —
  St. Ferdinand ....May 30

EUCHARISTIC ASSOCIATIONS
  AND CONGRESSES —
  St. Pascal Baylon ....May 17

FALSELY ACCUSED —
  St. Gerard Majella ....Oct. 16

FARMERS —
  St. Isidore ....May 15

FIRE PREVENTION —
  St. Catherine of Sienna..April 30

FISHERMEN —
  St. Andrew ....Nov. 30

FLORISTS —
  St. Dorothy ....Feb. 6

FLOUR INDUSTRY WORKERS—
  St. Arnulph ....Aug. 15

FUNERAL DIRECTORS —
  St. Joseph of
  Arimathea .... March 17

GARDENERS —
  St. Dorothy .... Feb. 6

GIRL SCOUTS —
  St. Agnes ....Jan. 21

GLASS INDUSTRY WORKERS—
  St. Luke ....Oct. 18

GREETINGS —
  St. Valentine ....Feb. 14

GROCERS —
  St. Michael ....Sept. 29

HATTERS & MILLINERISTS —
  St. Severus of Ravenna..Feb. 1

HOSPITALS —
  St. Camillus de Lellis ......July 18

HOUSEKEEPERS and
  HOUSEWIVES —
  St. Anne ....July 26

HUNTERS —
  St. Hubert ....Nov. 3

HOTEL INDUSTRY
  WORKERS —
  St. Amandus ....Feb. 6

INVALIDS —
  St. Roch ....Aug. 16

JEWELERS —
  St. Eligius ....Dec. 1

JOURNALISTS —
  St. Frances de Sales ....Jan. 29

LABORERS —
  St. Isidore ....April 4

LAWYERS —
  St. Ives ....May 19

LEATHER INDUSTRY
  WORKERS —
  SS. Crispan & Crispanian..Oct. 25

LIBRARIANS —
  St. Jerome ....Sept. 30

LOCKSMITHS —
  St. Dunstan ....May 19

LOVERS —
  St. Raphael ....Oct. 24

MERCHANTS —
St. Francis of Assisi ....Oct. 4

MESSENGERS —
St. Gabriel ....March 24

METAL WORKERS —
St. Eligius ....Dec. 1

MIDWIVES & OBSTETRICIANS
St. Raymond Nonnatus ....Aug. 31

MINERS —
St. Barbara ....Dec. 4

MISSIONS —
St. Francis Xavier ....Dec. 3

MUSICIANS —
St. Cecelia ....Nov. 22

MOTORCYCLISTS —
Our Lady of Grace ....Dec. 12

MOUNTAINEERS (Skiers?) —
St. Bernard of Menthon..May 28

NEGRO MISSIONS —
St. Peter Claver ....Sept. 8

NURSES —
St. Camillus de Lellis......July 18

OLD MAIDS —
St. Andrew ....Nov. 30

ORATORS —
St. John Chrysostom ....Jan. 27

ORPHANS AND DESERTED
CHILDREN —
St. Jerome Aemiliani ......July 20

PAINTERS —
St. Luke ....Oct. 18

PHILOSOPHERS —
St. Catherine of
Alexandria .... Nov. 25

PHYSICIANS —
SS. Cosmas & Damian....Sept. 27

PILGRIMS —
St. Alexius ....July 17

PLASTERERS —
St. Bartholomew ....Aug. 24

POETS —
St. David ....Dec. 29

POOR —
St. Lawrence ....Aug. 10

PORTERS —
St. Christopher ....July 25

POSTAL EMPLOYEES —
St. Gabriel ....March 24

PREGNANT WOMEN —
St. Gerard Majella ....Oct. 16

PRINTERS —
St. John of God ....March 8

PRISONERS —
St. Barbara ....Dec. 4

RETREATS —
St. Ignatius Loyola ....July 31

SAILORS —
St. Brendan ....May 16

SCHOOLS —
St. Thomas Aquinas ....March 7

SCIENTISTS —
St. Albert the Great ....Nov. 15

SCULPTORS —
St. Claude ....Nov. 8

SEAFARERS —
St. Michael ....Sept. 29

SHOEMAKERS —
SS. Crispan & Crispanian..Oct. 25

SICK —
St. Camillus de Lellis ....July 18

SINGERS —
St. Gregory ....March 12

SOLDIERS —
St. Sebastian ....Jan. 20

STEEL INDUSTRY
WORKERS —
St. Eligius ....Dec. 1

STENOGRAPHERS —
St. Genesius ....**Aug. 25**

STONESETTERS —
St. Stephen ....Dec. 26

STUDENTS —
St. Thomas Aquinas ....March 7

SURGEONS —
SS. Cosmas & Damian....Sept. 27

TAILORS —
St. Boniface of Credtion..June 5

TAX COLLECTORS —
St. Matthew ....Sept. 21

TEACHERS —
St. Gregory the Great..March 12

THEOLOGIANS —
St. Augustine ....Aug. 28

TIN WORKERS —
St. Joseph of
Arimathea .... March 17

TRAVELERS —
St. Christopher ....July 25

TRUCK DRIVERS —
St. Christopher ....July 25

TUITION-FREE SCHOOLS —
St. Joseph Calesanctius ..Aug. 27

UNIVERSAL CHURCH —
St. Joseph ....March 19

WINEGROWERS —
St. Vincent ....Jan. 22

WINESELLERS —
St. Amand ....Feb. 6

WOMEN IN LABOR —
St. Anne ....July 26

WORKINGMEN OF ALL
KINDS —
St. Joseph ....March 19

YOUTH —
GIRLS—St. Agnes ....Jan. 21
BOYS—St. Aloysius ....June 21

PATRON SAINTS

Our Lady of Lourdes is invoked against all bodily ills.

By long established devotion the following saints
are invoked against:

Apoplexy and Sudden Death ....St. Andrew Avellino
Arthritis & Rheumatism....St. James
Bite of Dogs ....St. Hubert
Bite of Snakes ....St. Hilary
Bruises ....St. Amalberga
Cancer ....St. Peregrine
Colic ....St. Agapitus
Consumption ....St. Pantaleon
Convulsion in Children ....
.... St. Scholastica
Cramps ....St. Maurice
Deafness ....St. Cadoc
Diseases of Breast ....St. Agatha
Diseases of Eye ....St. Lucy
Diseases of Throat ....St. Blase
Diseases of Tongue ....
........St. Catherine of Alexandria
Drought ....St. Eulalia
Dying without Sacraments ....
.....................St. Stanislaus Kostka
Earthquakes ....St. Francis Borgia
Epilepsy and Nervousness..St. Vitus
Exposure to Severe Cold ....
.... St. Genesius
Family Troubles ......St. Eustachius

Fever ....St. George
Fire ....St. Lawrence
Floods ....St. Columban
Foot Diseases ....St. Victor
Gall Stones ....St. Liberius
Glandular Disorders ....St. Cadoc
Gout ....St. Andrew
Hazards of Travel..St. Christopher
Headaches ....St. Denis
Insanity ....St. Dympna
Insects .... St. Tryphon
Intestinal Disorders ....St. Erasmus
Lightning, Thunder Storms & Fire
.... St. Barbara
Lumbago ....St. Lawrence
Paralysis ....St. Servelus
Pestilence .... St. Hadrian
Plague .... St. Casimir
Poisoning ....St. Benedict Nursia
Skin Diseases ....St. Roch
Sterility ....St. Giles
Stomach Disorders ....St. Lupus
Temptation at Hour of Death ....
.... St. Cyriacus
Toothache ....St. Apollonia
Typhus and Fevers ....St. Adalard

By long established devotion the following saints are invoked:

FOR THE GRACE OF A HAPPY DEATH ....St. Joseph
FOR THE RECOVERY OF LOST ARTICLES ......St. Anthony of Padua
FOR PERSEVERANCE IN PRAYER ....St. Monica
FOR THE APPREHENSION OF THIEVES ....SS. Gervase and Protase
FOR THE GRACE OF A GOOD CONFESSION ....St. Giles
TO OBTAIN A GOOD HUSBAND ....St. Joseph
TO OBTAIN A GOOD WIFE ....St. Anne
BY THOSE WHO WISH TO HAVE CHILDREN ....St. Felicitas

WHAT PARENTS SHOULD KNOW ABOUT THE BAPTISM OF THEIR CHILDREN

Baptism is the most important of the Sacraments, in the sense that it must be received before one is able to receive any of the others. Without it, in fact or desire, no one can enter heaven. By it .

1) We are freed from the original sin inherited from our first parents,—Adam and Eve.

2) We become Christians, participants in all the great things Christ has communicated to mankind.

3) We become children of God, very dear to Him, in a special way.

4) We become heirs to the kingdom of heaven,—eternal happiness in the prescence of God.

It is a spectacular and holy achievement, that parents can co-operate with God in giving life and all its wondrous possibilities to their children, and through Baptism, open the gates of heaven and a life of spiritual beauty and richness to them. The reverse is true of those sorry creatures, married persons who deliberately refuse to transmit life, and all the meanings and possibilities which life holds, to others.

1) Infants should be baptized as soon as possible after birth.

2) In *no case* should more than a month elapse between birth and baptism. If the child cannot be brought to the Church with safety, the priest should be summoned for baptism in the home.

3) One god-parent is required. Two are permitted, and this is customary. The two may not be of the same sex. Never more than two sponsors. God-parent and sponsor are interchangeable terms, —two words with the same meaning.

4) If a sponsor who has agreed to act in this capacity cannot be present for the baptism, a proxy may act in his place.

5) The child must be baptized in the parish church of its parents.

6) The child should be brought to the church at the pre-scribed time,—and on time.

7) It is always better to notify the priest that a child is to be presented for baptism. In many places this is required by the pastor.

8) Care should be used in choosing a name. This booklet presents a most wide selection, and the foreword gives helpful suggestions.

9) In preparing a child for baptism the clothing about the neck should be loose, or readily loosened, to facilitate the anointing with one of the holy oils.

10) The father usually accompanies the infant and sponsors to the church. The mother and others are welcome, but their freedom to witness the baptism may be curtailed by a lack of space in the baptistry.

WHAT A GOD-PARENT SHOULD KNOW

By assuming this office a sponsor agrees to take a lasting interest in the life and spiritual welfare of the child. If the parents neglect, or are unable to provide for the Catholic education of the child, the sponsor must do so, as far as possible.

During the baptismal ceremony the sponsor, or sponsors, speak for the child.

The sponsor should be able to recite the Apostles Creed and the Our Father.

The sponsor should feel no nervousness or apprehension. The priest will give the necessary directions and suggest the proper answers. The description of the ceremonies, as given below, will be of great help, and may be brought to the church for that purpose.

REQUIREMENTS FOR SPONSORS

To act validly, a sponsor must be baptized and have attained the use of reason and have the intention of being a sponsor. He must not belong to an heretical or schismatic sect, nor have been excommunicated, nor suffer from infamy of law, nor be excluded from legal acts. He may not be the father, mother or spouse of the one to be baptized. He must be designated by the child's parents, or by guardians, or in their default by the minister of baptism. The sponsor must hold or touch the infant or receive it immediately after baptism from the hands of the priest.

For lawful sponsorship, the god-parent must be fourteen years of age, unless for a just cause, when one younger may be admitted. He should know the rudiments of Catholic doctrine. He must not be notoriously excommunicated, nor have lost his good name. Without permission of his proper Superior, a member of a religious community or one in Sacred Orders, cannot act as sponsor. Since the god-parent has a spiritual obligation toward the child, those best informed in the Faith and most exact in Its practice are to be preferred as sponsors.

WHAT THE SPONSOR SHOULD KNOW ABOUT THE CEREMONY OF BAPTISM

Before the ceremony, for the church records, the sponsors should be able to supply the following information:

a) The name to be given the infant.

b) The names of the parents, including the maiden name of the mother.

c) The date of birth.

Besides the actual pouring of the water, accompanied by the necessary words, there are a number of other ceremonies and prayers. These do not directly concern the sponsors. The following treatment of the ceremonies is designed to help the sponsors understand and fulfill their role in the administration of the sacrament.

The priest addresses the infant and the sponsors answer for it.

Priest: N................what dost thou ask of the Church of God?

Sponsor: Faith.

Priest: What does faith bring to thee?

Sponsor: Life everlasting.

Several ceremonies and prayers follow, in the last of which he places the stole upon the shoulder of the child, as leading it into the church, saying;

N................enter into the temple of God, that thou mayest have part with Christ, unto life everlasting. Amen.

He then tells the sponsors to recite aloud the Apostles Creed and the Our Father.

APOSTLES CREED

I believe in God the Father almighty, Creator of heaven and earth. And in Jesus Christ, His only Son, our Lord, who was conceived by the Holy Ghost, born of the Virgin Mary, suffered

nder Pontius Pilate, was crucified, died and was buried. He
escended into hell, the third day He rose again from the dead, He
scended into heaven, and sitteth at the right hand of God the
'ather almighty; from thence He shall come to judge the living
nd the dead. I believe in the Holy Ghost, the holy Catholic
Church, the communion of saints, the forgiveness of sins, the
esurrection of the body, and life everlasting. Amen.

OUR FATHER

Our Father, who art in heaven, hallowed be thy name. Thy
kingdom come. Thy will be done on earth, as it is in heaven.
Give us this day our daily bread. And forgive us our trespasses,
as we forgive those who trespass against us. And lead us not into
temptation, but deliver us from evil. Amen.

A prayer and a ceremony follow; after which the priest addresses
the infant.

Priest: N................dost thou renounce Satan?

Sponsor: I do renounce him.

Priest: And all his works?

Sponsor: I do renounce them.

Priest: And all his pomps?

Sponsor: I do renounce them.

Here the child is anointed on the breast and between the
shoulders with the Oil of Catechumens, in the form of a cross.
The sponsors can assist by holding the garments away from these
places while the priest anoints and then wipes the oil away.

The priest again addresses the infant and the sponsors reply.

Priest: N................, dost thou believe in God the Father almighty, Creator of heaven and earth?

Sponsor: I do believe.

Priest: Dost thou believe in Jesus Christ, His only Son, our
Lord, who was born and who suffered for us?

Sponsor: I do believe.

Priest: Dost thou believe also in the Holy Ghost, the holy
Catholic Church, the Communion of saints, the forgiveness of sins,
the resurrection of the body, and the life everlasting?

Sponsor: I do believe.

Priest : N................, wilt thou be baptized.

Sponsor: I will.

While one sponsor holds the child and the other places h
hand on it, the priest takes baptismal water and pours it thr
times in the form of a cross, on the head of the child, saying
the same time :

N......................., I BAPTIZE THEE, IN THE NAM
OF THE FATHER, AND OF THE SON, AND OF TH
HOLY GHOST.

The priest anoints the head of the child with Holy Chrism
as though sealing the baptism. He then places a white cloth, sym
bolic of the purity of life which should follow. A lighted candl
is given the sponsors to hold while the final prayer is recite
The ceremony is concluded with the priest saying to the baptized

N................, go in peace, and the Lord be with you. Amen

At this point it is customary to make an offering. The amoun
is determined by diocesan statute or local custom. The child i
then returned to its home.

EMERGENCY BAPTISM

Under ordinary circumstances, Baptism should be administered
only by a priest. However, if the infant is in danger of death, and
a priest is not readily available, a lay-person can and should baptize.
A qualified sponsor should be had if possible. If holy water is not
available, natural water will suffice. The water must *flow* on
the head of the child. Every foetus born prematurely, every
miscarriage, no matter at what stage of pregnancy, must be
baptized. If it is not certain that life is present, baptism is given
conditionally, i.e. "If you are living I baptise thee etc." Water
is to be poured on the head or if this is not possible, upon any
rcognizable human part.

The baptism is performed by pouring the water upon the head :
and *while pouring* say, in an audible voice; "I BAPTIZE THEE
IN THE NAME OF THE FATHER, AND OF THE SON,
AND OF TE HOLY GHOST."

REGISTER

Name Aaron David Salazar

Date of Birth 9-9-09 Date of Baptism 2-14-10

Name ....

Date of Birth .... Date of Baptism ....

Name ....

Date of Birth .... Date of Baptism ....

Name ....

Date of Birth .... Date of Baptism ....

Name ....

Date of Birth .... Date of Baptism ....

Name ....

Date of Birth .... Date of Baptism ....